PASSPORT TO

ISRAEL

Clive A. Lawton

Franklin Watts

London/New York/Sydney/Toronto

Copyright © 1987 Franklin Watts Limited

First published in Great Britain by
Franklin Watts Limited
12a Golden Square
London W1R 4BA

First published in the USA by
Franklin Watts Inc.
387 Park Avenue South
New York
NY 10016

First published in Australia by
Franklin Watts Australia
14 Mars Road
Lane Cove
NSW 2066

UK ISBN: 0 86313 534 X
US ISBN: 0-531-10494-X
Library of Congress Catalog Card No: 87-50891

Editors: Theodore Rowland-Entwistle
        Jean Cooke
Design: Edward Kinsey
Illustrations: Hayward Art Group
Consultant: Keith Lye

Photographs: Sonia Halliday
Photographs/Barrie Searle 8T, 8B, 9TL,
9TR, 9CL, 9LR, 16T, 16B, 17T, 17B, 18B,
19TL, 19B, 20T, 20B, 21T, 21B, 22T,
24T, 24B, 29TL, 29TR, 30T, 33TR,
33B, 34T, 34B, 35T, 38B, 39B, 41TL;
Sonia Halliday Photographs/Lushington
9CR, 10B, 11B, 13T, 19TR, 31B, 38T;
Sonia Halliday Photographs/Taylor 39T,
45B; Sonia Halliday Photographs 6B,
10T, 12T, 18T, 29B; BIPAC 22B, 23TL,
23TR, 23B, 25TL, 25TR, 25B, 35B, 40T,
40BL, 42T, 42B, 43T, 43B, 44BL, 44BR,
45TL; Popperfoto 45TR; Y. Rubin 41B; V.
Silver 40BR; Zefa 5T, 5B, 6T, 7T, 7B, 9B,
11T, 13B, 28T, 28B, 30B, 31TL, 31TR,
32B, 33TL, 44T.

Front cover: Sonia Halliday Photographs/Barry Searle
Back cover: Sonia Halliday Photographs

Phototypeset by Keyspools Limited
Colour reproduction by Hongkong Graphic Arts
Printed in Belgium

Contents

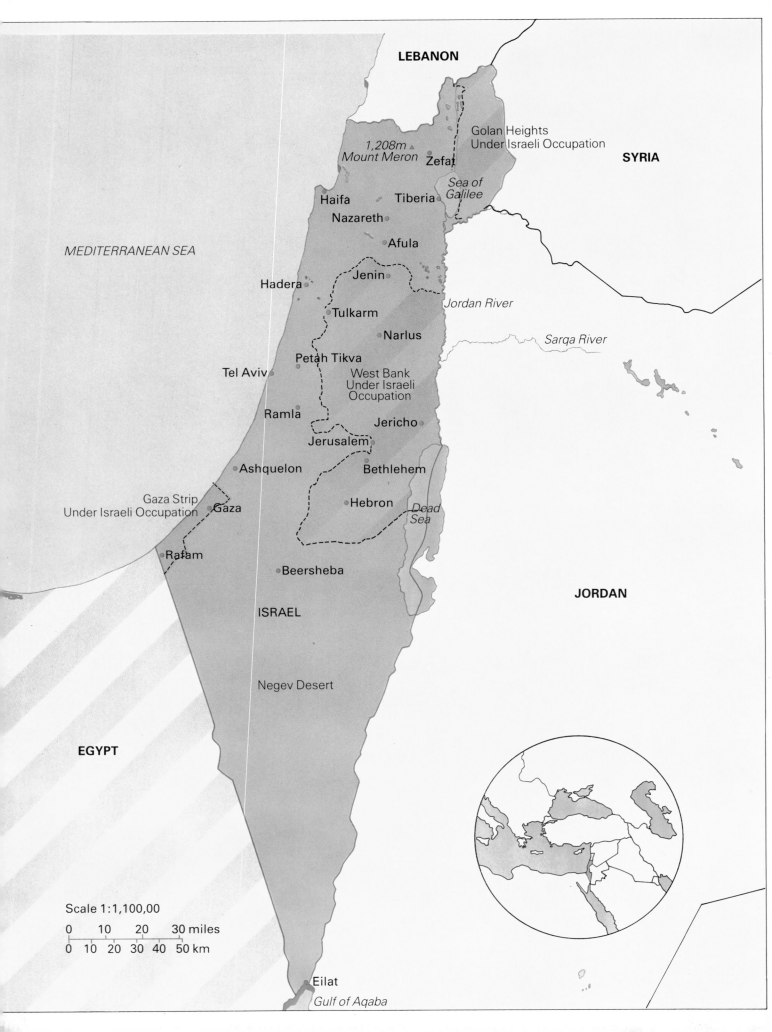

LEBANON

SYRIA

Golan Heights
Under Israeli Occupation

1,208m ▲
Mount Meron

Zefat

*Sea of
Galilee*

Haifa
Tiberia

Nazareth

Afula

MEDITERRANEAN SEA

Hadera
Jenin

Tulkarm
Jordan River

Narlus
Sarqa River

Petah Tikva

Tel Aviv
West Bank
Under Israeli
Occupation

Ramla
Jericho

Jerusalem

Ashquelon
Bethlehem

Gaza Strip
Under Israeli Occupation
Gaza
Hebron
*Dead
Sea*

Rafam

Beersheba
JORDAN

ISRAEL

Negev Desert

EGYPT

Scale 1:1,100,00

0   10   20   30 miles

0 10 20 30 40 50 km

Eilat
Gulf of Aqaba

Introduction

Israel is one of the world's most remarkable nations. In one sense it is an old country, and the origins of its culture and many of its towns go back thousands of years. In another way, it is a new country, founded in 1948. Its people include many immigrants – Jews from all over the world, speaking different languages, who have returned to their homeland. Under threat from the Arab world, the Israelis have been learning to become one people. With determination and resourcefulness they have improved their technology, particularly in agriculture and land reclamation, and so made their small country the most developed in the Middle East.

Israel lies at a cultural crossroads where Asia joins Africa. It also has historic links with Europe and the rest of the Western world. It is a place of great importance to three of the world's major religions, Judaism, Christianity and Islam, and many people call it The Holy Land. For this reason hundreds of thousands of pilgrims visit Israel every year.

Above: Israel is a great mixture of different peoples and cultures. Here a group of black-clad Hasidic Jews walk through a colorful Arab souk (open-air market) in Jerusalem.

Below: The modern face of Israel is shown clearly in this view of Tel Aviv from the 32nd floor of the Shalom Tower. The city is Israel's industrial and commercial center.

The land

Israel is a long, narrow country, about 435 km (270 miles) from north to south and 110 km (68 miles) from east to west. It lies at the eastern end of the Mediterranean Sea, and has four Arab countries on its borders: Lebanon, Syria, Jordan and Egypt. It has an outlet to the Gulf of Aqaba, an arm of the Red Sea, in the south, where the port of Eilat is located.

The Mediterranean coast has extensive sandy beaches, with seaside resorts that attract not only many tourists but also Israelis, particularly on weekends. In the far northwest the coastline becomes more rocky and hilly, creating the beautiful grottoes and caves of Rosh Hanikra.

The Negev desert is a huge triangle occupying southern Israel, and tapering southwards to the port of Eilat on the Gulf of Aqaba. Eilat is a popular seaside resort. It has an underwater national park where tropical fish can be seen through the clear seawater.

Above: Galilee is a green and fertile land, with a more temperate climate than the rest of Israel. The River Jordan, Israel's small but most important river, runs through it.

Below: A Bedouin girl tends sheep in the Negev Desert. Israel's apparently barren deserts provide grazing for the flocks that are kept by the Bedouin.

Within Israel are two lakes or seas. The Sea of Galilee (also called Lake Tiberias or Lake Kinneret) in the north is a freshwater lake fed by the River Jordan. The Jordan, Israel's longest river, eventually flows into the Dead Sea, the world's saltiest lake. The bottom of the Dead Sea is the floor of the Great Rift Valley, a huge split in the Earth's crust which extends from Syria to Mozambique in southern Africa. The sea's shoreline is the world's lowest point on land. The sea is called "Dead" because it is so full of salt and other minerals that nothing can live in it.

Northeast Israel contains the Judeo-Galilean Highlands. Jerusalem, the capital, lies further south among the Judean Hills on the border with Jordan.

Israel's summers are hot and dry and the winters are generally mild. Most of the rain falls in winter, and central and northern Israel sometimes have snow. When rain falls in the barren-looking southern desert, plants hidden in the ground spring to life, bloom quickly and die as the land dries out again.

Above: The Golan Heights lie on the border between Israel and Syria. From these mountains, Syria used to shell northern Israeli settlements. Israel captured them in 1967.

Below: The Dead Sea is so salty that it is impossible even for non-swimmers to sink. The salts include potash, bromides and magnesium salts, which are important mineral resources.

The people

Israel has two main groups of people: Jews and Arabs, so it has two official languages: Hebrew and Arabic. Many Israelis speak both languages and English. By 1980 four-fifths of the people were Jews, many of whom were immigrants, and most of the rest were Arabs.

Israel's complex population is the result of its turbulent history. For thousands of years people have fought to control the land because of its importance as a gateway between Asia and Africa. The Hebrews, the ancestors of the Jews, arrived there nearly 4,000 years ago. The Jews take their name from the Kingdom of Judah, founded about 900 BC. They were successively overrun by Assyrians, Babylonians, Persians, Greeks and Romans.

Finally, after an unsuccessful revolt against the Romans in the 2nd century AD, most of the Jews were driven from the land in what is known as the Diaspora, the "scattering". The Diaspora was virtually complete by the 5th century AD.

Above: A typical Arab family group. The older members wear clothing of Middle Eastern style, but the children's clothes are similar to Western ones.

Below: An Orthodox Jewish family enjoys the sunshine on a park bench in Jerusalem. On warm days Israelis tend to dress informally.

Above: A policeman guards the Knesset.

Below: Most girls serve in the defense forces.

Above: An assistant serves in a supermarket.

Below: An Armenian Patriarch.

After the prophet Muhammad founded the Islamic religion in the 7th century AD his followers, the Muslim Arabs, occupied Israel, so Israel is a holy place for Muslims as well as for Christians and Jews. Christians revere it as the land where Jesus of Nazareth lived. In the 1100s and 1200s Christians from Europe tried to win back the land from the Muslims – whom they called Saracens – in a series of wars known as the Crusades. The few Jews living there at that time were powerless. The Christian armies were finally driven out by the Saracens. From the early 1500s the region became part of the Ottoman (Turkish) Empire, which was Muslim.

Only at the end of the 19th century did the Jews start to believe that they could be independent again in the land of their ancestors. Since 1948, when the modern country of Israel was founded, about 2 million immigrants have settled there. Just under half have come from Europe and America. The others – the so-called Oriental Jews – have come from Asia or Africa.

Above: A Moroccan Jew wears his traditional dress.

Below: A Bedouin of the Negev leans on his camel.

Where people live

Israel has a population of over four million. About 1,280,000 more people live in the disputed territories occupied by Israel – Judea and Samaria on the west bank of the River Jordan, the Gaza strip near Egypt in the southwest, and the Golan Heights bordering Syria in the northeast. Most Israelis live along the Mediterranean coast.

Most of Israel's industry is located around the coastal cities. Three in every hundred Israelis choose to live in a kibbutz. "Kibbutz" (plural "kibbutzim") means a group. Kibbutzim are agricultural or industrial settlements. They give an important clue to understanding how the Israelis have settled and developed the land over the past hundred years, and how they see themselves as pioneers. The people of the kibbutz live together as a community, sharing work and meals. In some kibbutzim the children live together in a separate house, creating a different sort of society.

Above: Nazareth was the village where Jesus spent his boyhood. Today it is a bustling town of more than 35,000 people. The Church of the Annunciation is on the traditional site of Jesus's home.

Left: An aerial view of Sede Boker Kibbutz, in southern Israel. The carefully tended fields of the kibbutzim provide Israel not only with much of its food, but with crops for export.

Judea and Samaria, and the northern area of Galilee, are dotted with small towns and villages. Most people there are Arabs; some are Muslims and others are Christians. Other Arabs live in the cities. One in ten of all Israelis live in Jerusalem.

Some Arabs follow the Jewish religion. Most of them live in the new towns that have grown up in the past 40 years. These towns were founded to provide homes for the enormous numbers of immigrants. Israel encouraged this immigration problem by declaring that all Jews were welcome. The immigrants include Jews from Arab lands escaping persecution, and those from Central Europe escaping from the Holocaust – the mass killing of European Jews during World War II – or from its memories. Many other Jews have come to Israel to help build up the homeland, bringing with them a variety of skills and talents from all regions of the world. Israel's population has increased by nearly five times since 1948 although the rate of population growth slowed considerably during the 1980s.

Above: The ancient port of Akko (Acre) on the shores of the Mediterranean is now a quiet town, but in the Middle Ages it was a main port for trade between Asia and Europe.

Below: A new housing development at Ramot, north of Jerusalem. The need for 25,000 new homes every year supports a thriving construction industry.

Jerusalem

The capital city of Jerusalem is in central Israel. It was the country's capital under King David nearly 3,000 years ago, and his son King Solomon built the first Jewish temple in the city. Because Jerusalem stands high in the Judean hills it has no natural water supply. One of ancient Israel's great engineering feats was to cut a long tunnel through rock to bring a supply of drinking water into the city.

Jerusalem is a focus of worship and interest for three great religions. The Western (or Wailing) Wall is the last remaining part of the Jewish temple which the Romans destroyed more than 1,900 years ago. For centuries Jews have gathered beside it to pray. The city is especially holy for Christians because it is the place where Jesus of Nazareth was crucified. The Church of the Holy Sepulchre stands on what is believed to be the Calvary, where Jesus died. Muslims regard Jerusalem as holy because it contains the place from which Muhammad is believed to have visited Heaven and spoken with God; the spot is marked by the beautiful Dome of the Rock.

Above: The Damascus Gate leads into the Old City of Jerusalem from the north. The gate and walls were built in the 1500s.

Below: The map shows the location of the principal buildings of Jerusalem, such as the Dome of the Rock.

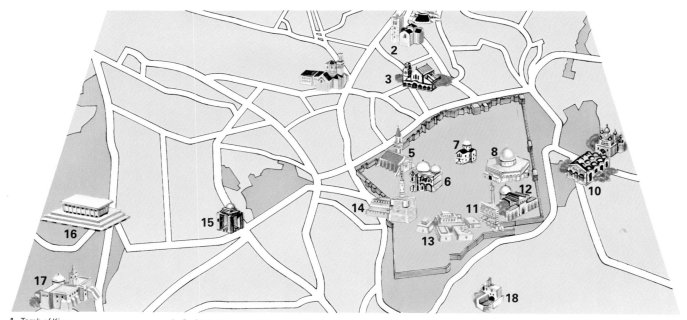

1. Tomb of Kings
2. St. George Cathedral
3. St. Stephen's Basilica
4. Italian Hospital
5. St. Savior
6. Church of the Holy Sepulchre
7. Armenian Cathedral Patriarchate
8. Dome of the Rock
9. St. Mary Magdalen
10. Gethsemane Basilica of Agony
11. Hakotel Hammaravi (Western Wall)
12. El Aqsa Mosque
13. Yeshivat Porat Yosef
14. David's Tower
15. Heichal Shlomo
16. Knesset
17. Monastery of the Cross
18. Pool of Siloam

Other landmarks include the Knesset, Israel's parliament building; the Old City, whose walls were built by the Ottoman Turks in the 1600s; and the New City which has grown up in the past hundred years.

The Old City is divided into Armenian, Christian, Jewish and Muslim quarters. When Israel was founded in 1948 Jerusalem was divided. The Old City to the east was part of Jordan, and the New City in the west was in Israel. Since the Six-Day War in 1967 Jerusalem has been united under Israeli rule. The Israeli government has built roads between the Old and New parts and allows Jews, Christians and Muslims to have free access to their holy places. More than a million pilgrims and tourists flock there every year. Jerusalem is one of the world's most multicultural and multiracial cities. All the buildings in Jerusalem are faced with the warm yellow local stone, making it "Jerusalem the Golden".

Above: An aerial view of the Temple area of Jerusalem, the heart of the Old City. The Dome of the Rock is a Muslim shrine.

Below: For Jews the Western Wall in Jerusalem is one of the most holy places. It is part of the Temple built by Herod.

Fact file : land and population

Key facts

Location: Israel borders the eastern shore of the Mediterranean Sea in south-western Asia. It lies roughly between latitudes 29°30′ and 33°15′ North, and longitudes 34°15′ and 35°40′ East.

Main parts: Israel is divided into six districts: Central, Haifa, Jerusalem, Northern, Southern and Tel Aviv. Jerusalem includes East Jerusalem, which was under Jordanian rule before the 1967 Six-Day War.

Area: 20,770 sq km (8,019 sq miles). This does not include any of the disputed territories – the Gaza Strip, the Golan Heights and the West Bank of the Jordan.

Population: 4,150,000 (1984 estimate).

Capital: Jerusalem.

Major cities and towns:
Jerusalem (473,000)
Tel Aviv-Jaffa (327,000)
Haifa (575,000)
Beersheba (479,000)

Languages: Hebrew and Arabic are the official languages. Other languages are spoken by immigrants. Between 1948 and 1984, about 1,758,000 immigrants settled in Israel. Some 79.5 per cent came from Europe and North America, while 20 per cent, the so-called Oriental Jews, came from Africa and Asia. Hebrew is the language used in Jewish schools and Arabic in Arab/Druze schools, but many Israelis are bilingual.

Highest point: Mount Meron, in the far north, 1,208 m (3,963 ft). Mount Hermon, an ancient landmark on the border between the Israeli-held Golan Heights and Lebanon, is 2,810 m (9,220 ft).

Lowest point: The shoreline of the Dead Sea in the Rift Valley is 400 m (1,312 ft) below sea level. This is the world's lowest point on land.

Longest river: River Jordan, which has headstreams in Syria and Lebanon. It empties into the Dead Sea. Total length: about 320 km (200 miles).

Area: 1,040 sq km (401 sq miles).

Largest lake: Dead Sea, which lies partly in Israel and partly in Jordan.

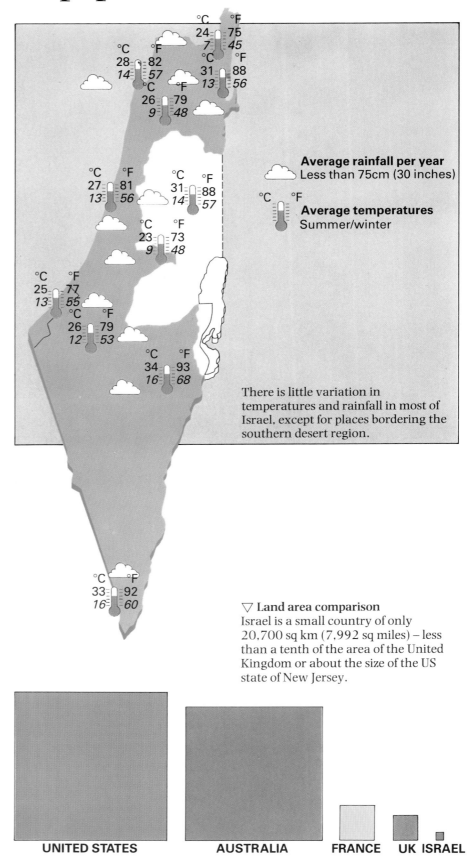

Average rainfall per year Less than 75cm (30 inches)

Average temperatures Summer/winter

There is little variation in temperatures and rainfall in most of Israel, except for places bordering the southern desert region.

▽ **Land area comparison**
Israel is a small country of only 20,700 sq km (7,992 sq miles) – less than a tenth of the area of the United Kingdom or about the size of the US state of New Jersey.

UNITED STATES **AUSTRALIA** **FRANCE** **UK ISRAEL**

▽ Major population centers
Apart from Jerusalem, most major Israeli cities are along the west coast, bordering the Mediterranean Sea, linked by a coast road and railroad.

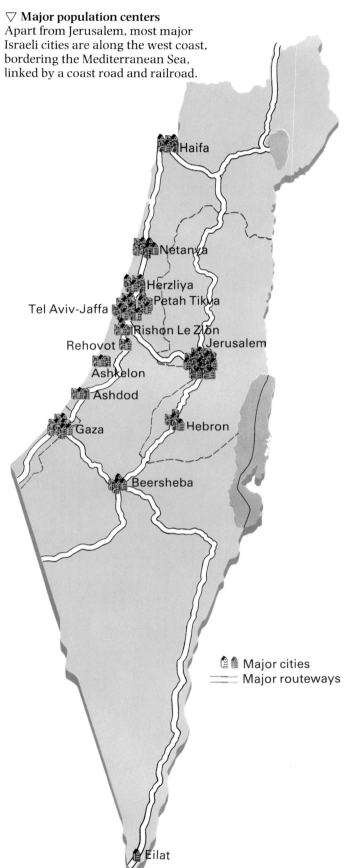

Haifa
Netanya
Herzliya
Petah Tikva
Tel Aviv-Jaffa
Rishon Le Zion
Rehovot
Jerusalem
Ashkelon
Ashdod
Gaza
Hebron
Beersheba
Eilat

🏠🏠 Major cities
═══ Major routeways

◁ Where people live
Most people in Israel have an urban lifestyle, with nine times as many people living in towns and cities as in the country districts.

Urban 90% **Rural** 10%

▽ A population density comparison
Israel is a fairly crowded country, with a population density twice as high as France and nearly as high as the United Kingdom.

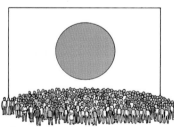

United Kingdom
231 per sq km

Japan
320 per sq km

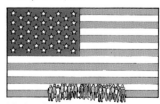

Australia
2 per sq km

United States
25 per sq km

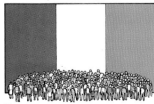

France
100 per sq km

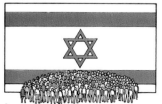

Israel
200 per sq km

Home life

Nearly all Israelis live in high-rise apartments, rather than houses. The people living in an apartment often share the responsibility of looking after the building. They elect committees to run the building and allocate the various tasks needed to keep it clean and in good repair.

A typical Israeli family home consists of a living room, which also serves as a dining room. There is a small kitchen, a balcony, a bathroom with a toilet, and some bedrooms. Children often have to share rooms, and because space in most apartments is limited bunk beds are very popular.

Floors are usually tiled to keep rooms cool in summer, but heating is needed in Jerusalem because the winters there can be chilly, and snow sometimes falls. By contrast, air conditioning is necessary on the coastal plain, because it is often extremely humid there in the summer months.

Above: The oasis town of Beersheba provides more space than in other towns, so families can have their own houses rather than the apartments in which four out of five Israelis live.

Below: The main living room of the house in Beersheba is cool and spacious. It is typical of living-rooms in many Israeli homes, including those in kibbutzim.

The Israelis' homes are always open to neighbors and other visitors. Social life is informal, and people visit one another without making any arrangements in advance. There are many Jewish festivals which provide a regular excuse for large family gatherings. Most households own a television set, but families often spend their evenings playing games together, singing songs or just chatting.

When Israelis meet they greet each other with the word "Shalom," which means "peace." Shalom is used for both "Hello" and "Goodbye."

The strictest orthodox Jews are careful to keep Shabat (the Sabbath). It lasts from sunset on Friday evening to sunset on Saturday, and during that period they avoid working day activities. Many families, even those that are not particularly religious, tend to gather together on Friday evening to share their main meal of the week. Muslim Israelis keep their Sabbath on Fridays, and Christians have theirs on Sundays. Some Israelis do not observe Shabbat.

Above: A Jewish mother in an apartment in Jerusalem teaches her young son to read. Space is limited in most Israeli homes, so bunk beds are popular for children to sleep in.

Below: Hanukkah, the Festival of Lights, is a Jewish festival. Each day for eight days the family lights a candle in the menorah, or candelabrum, until all eight are lit.

Shops and shopping

Israelis do most of their shopping in small stores, although the largest cities and towns have big department stores, and the number of supermarkets is gradually increasing. When shopping for food, Israelis usually prefer fresh produce to canned or packaged food, although the long hours that men and women work leaves them little time for cooking. Israel's farms produce about 60 per cent of its food.

Shops in Israel are generally open every day, except Saturday, between 8 a.m. and 7 p.m., but they close for a long break during the hottest part of the day, between 12.30 p.m. and 2.30 p.m. They close early on Friday evenings in preparation for Shabbat. Closing days differ in Christian and Muslim areas to suit the main religious communities there, who observe different Sabbath days.

Tel Aviv has the best shops, which have a range and quality of goods equal to those in any western capital. One Tel Aviv shop has started to open 24 hours a day, though it closes for Shabbat.

Above: An Arab trader selling fabrics in the market at Beersheba. The wares are displayed on the ground. Israelis enjoy shopping at markets and in small shops.

Below: The Supersol supermarket in Jerusalem. Supermarkets make shopping easier for many Israeli families where both husband and wife work full time.

Traditional craftware is available in many of the ancient cities, such as Jerusalem, Jaffa and Safed. In Arab markets, small open-fronted shops called *souks*, classical styles of Arab clothing, jewellery and trinkets are displayed side by side with modern western fashions. Many are in old, narrow streets that are too narrow for cars. No prices are fixed in these markets. The first price quoted by the seller is only the start of a long and often entertaining ritual of bargaining, which sometimes puzzles tourists but is a traditional part of Middle Eastern life.

People who live on a kibbutz have little need for shops, because everything is provided by the kibbutz in return for their labor. The kibbutzniks, as the people of a kibbutz are often called, neither earn wages nor pay directly for their food, clothing and vacations. However, many kibbutzim have a small general store which provides little items that people might desire for their personal use.

Above left: Most Israelis prefer to buy fresh vegetables and fruit rather than canned goods.

Above right: Tourist shops display Arab craft wares in the Old City of Jerusalem.

Below: A Jerusalem butcher prepares meat. Many Jews only eat meat which is kosher, that is, slaughtered and prepared in accordance with strict Jewish religious laws.

Cooking and eating

So many of Israel's people have come from widely differing national backgrounds that it is usual to find restaurants in one town that serve American, Chinese, French, Greek, Hungarian, Indian, Iraqi, Italian, Moroccan, Turkish, Vietnamese and Yemeni foods, in addition to all the traditional foods popular with the Arabs and Jews.

All public buildings and many restaurants are bound by kashrut, the dietary law of Judaism. The food they serve must be kosher, which means "ritually correct." Kashrut is based on ancient traditions, set down in the Bible. Certain meats are forbidden to orthodox Jews, especially pork, pork products such as sausages, and shellfish, such as clams or crabs. Because meat and milk products may not be cooked together or eaten at the same meal, most restaurants choose to serve either meat-based meals or meals that use fish and dairy foods. However, not all Israeli Jews observe kashrut strictly.

Above: For many Israelis breakfast is one of the most important meals of the day. Here the dishes for a typical Israeli breakfast are displayed at a hotel in Tel Aviv.

Below: For most people the main meal of the day is eaten at about 8 o'clock in the evening. It is very much a family occasion, and also a time for entertaining friends.

The most notable meal of the Israeli day is breakfast. This extensive meal includes vegetables, cheese, yogurt and often cooked dishes as well. Breakfast in an Israeli hotel is well worth having. The main "filler food" is not bread, potato or pasta, but rice, which Oriental Jews in particular cook in a variety of delicious ways.

Perhaps the most famous Israeli food is falafel. Falafel consists of little balls of ground chick peas or white beans, mixed with onions, garlic and spices and fried in oil. They are generally served in pockets of thin, soft pita bread, with a salad of chopped tomato and cucumber and various hot and spicy sauces. Falafel is sold in cafés and on stalls all over the country. It is an ancient Middle East tradition, and possibly the original "fast food."

Israelis eat large amounts of home-grown chicken and turkey. They enjoy ripe grapefruit, oranges and avocados – which do not travel well – but the best of the crop is mostly exported.

Above: Street stalls throughout Israel sell falafel to passers-by. Falafel is a traditional Middle Eastern delicacy, fried vegetable balls in pitta bread.

Below: A tourist menu is printed partly in Hebrew and partly in English for the benefit of visitors.

Pastimes and sport

Israelis work a six-day week, with Saturday as the main day off. Working hours are fairly long, and therefore people do not have a lot of leisure time. However, most Israelis are enthusiastic about sports.

Although Israel is a small country, it has become successful, particularly in chess, basketball and badminton. For example, Israel's Maccabi Tel-Aviv basketball team has won the European Cup twice. Every school has its own basketball pitch, and apartment buildings have basketball hoops attached to walls for youngsters to use. New housing developments generally have safe, attractive playgrounds for young children.

Soccer is growing increasingly popular. Many Israelis follow the fortunes of local soccer teams and the British soccer leagues as well. Israelis enjoy swimming, and the country is so small that most people do not live far from a beach. Tennis and golf are other favorite sports.

Above: A beach scene near Tel Aviv. Israel's Mediterranean coast has many sandy beaches, where the people like to spend their time fishing, playing games or just enjoying the sun.

Left: A tense moment in an international soccer match between Israel and Taiwan. Soccer is one of the most popular sports.

Above: The Israeli Maccabi Tel Aviv basketball team in action. This team has twice won the European Cup.

Right: A parachutist drops in to mark the opening of the 11th Maccabiah Games.

Below: The Eurovision Song Contest was held in Israel in 1979. Israel enters this international television contest every year, and has twice been the winner.

In athletics, Israel organizes the Maccabiah Games, on similar lines to the Olympic Games. They have been held every four years since 1932, and draw Jewish athletes from all over the world. Israel takes part in the Olympic Games.

Dancing and singing are extremely popular pastimes, and Israel has a strong folk tradition in both. Many young people at discos spend some time dancing to ordinary pop music and the rest performing folk dances from European and Middle Eastern cultures. The most popular folk dance is the hora.

Israel's folksongs are drawn from many traditions, some deeply rooted in Jewish lore, others coming from the countries of Eastern Europe where so many Jews lived. The country has its own pop singers, and has twice won the Eurovision Song Contest on television.

Israel is full of ancient historical places and archaeology is a national pastime. Many people give up free time to join in the excavation of interesting sites.

News and broadcasting

Above: A selection of Israeli newspapers and magazines. Fifteen newspapers are published in Hebrew and five in Arabic, plus nine in other languages.

Below: Newstands carry a wide variety of newspapers in several languages, and popular magazines on a variety of topics. Israeli publishers produce about 650 periodicals.

Israel has about 30 daily or weekly newspapers. Fifteen are in Hebrew and five in Arabic. The others are in a variety of languages including Yiddish, a European dialect spoken by millions of Jews in all parts of the world. The newspapers are without exception fairly literary and demanding: Israel has no real equivalent of the popular newspaper. In addition there are hundreds of periodicals and magazines covering all sorts of interests.

Interest in news is intense. Israelis listen keenly to the five radio stations of Kol Yisrael (The Voice of Israel). The stations are controlled by the Israel Broadcasting Authority, which is independent of the government and is modeled on the lines of the British Broadcasting Corporation. One station broadcasts entirely in Arabic for Arabic-speaking Israelis. Another runs regular features in a dozen different languages for the benefit of the large number of new immigrants who are always to be found in Israel.

Radio listening is so strong a habit that passengers commonly fall silent to listen to the news on the bus radio. They then break out in animated discussions about what they have heard.

The Israel Broadcasting Authority also runs the television service. About half the TV programs are made in Israel, particularly those concerned with news, politics and current affairs. Hebrew language programs sometimes carry subtitles in Arabic and Arabic items are subtitled in Hebrew. Many other programs come from the United States or Britain and carry subtitles in both Hebrew and Arabic. Many people also watch Jordanian television.

Israel has about a hundred publishers, who between them produce a thousand books each year. Many of the most successful books deal with matters of social concern in Israel, and are translated into other languages for sale on the home market and in other countries throughout the world.

Above left: David Broza, who sings and plays the guitar, is a popular TV personality.

Above right: The singer Ofra Haza frequently appears on TV and has made many recordings.

Below: Book fairs are popular attractions, such as the Hebrew Book Week held in Tel Aviv.

Fact file: home and leisure

Key facts

Population composition: In 1983 people under 15 years of age made up 32.1 per cent of the population; people aged between 15 and 59 made up 54.9 per cent; and people over 60 made up 13.0 per cent. Women formed 50.18 per cent of the population.

Average life expectancy at birth: 75 years in 1984, as compared with 71.5 years in 1965.

Rate of population increase: 2.2 per cent per year between 1973 and 1984, as compared with 3.1 per cent between 1965 and 1973. A lower rate of 1.7 per cent per year (roughly the world average) is forecast between 1980 and 2000.

Family life: The marriage rate in 1984 was 7 per 1,000 people. The average age when men marry is 27.6 years, and that for women is 23.9. The average size of urban households is 3.5 persons. More than 400,000 households have two or more wage-earners. As a rule, people take about 14 days' vacation a year, and there are also about 10 national holidays

Work: The total work force in 1985 was 1,456,000, of which women made up 34.7 per cent and men 65.3 per cent (5.9 per cent of the work force was unemployed). The average monthly income per household was US $762 (£522). The average weekly hours of work were 45 in offices and 50 in factories. Men between 21 and 55 spend one month each year on army service.

Prices: Prices rose by an average of 8.2 per cent a year between 1965 and 1973. Between 1973 and 1984 inflation averaged 84.4 per cent. In mid-1984 it soared to 400 per cent. By 1987 it was below 15 per cent.

Religion: The chief religion is Judaism, but Israel's Jews vary from those who are extremely Orthodox to those without religious beliefs. The law guarantees religious freedom. In 1985 Israel had 551,000 Muslims, 97,000 Christians and 69,000 Druzes

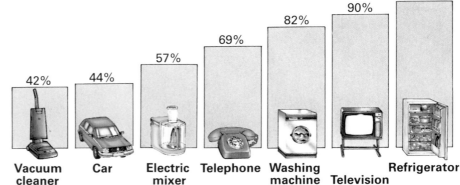

42%	44%	57%	69%	82%	90%	99%
Vacuum cleaner	Car	Electric mixer	Telephone	Washing machine	Television	Refrigerator

Transportation 2.9%
Fuel and light 4%
Clothing and footwear 4.5%

Housing and furnishing 26%

Food, beverages and tobacco 26.2%

Other goods and services 36.4%

△ **How many households owned goods in 1986**
Nearly all Israeli homes have a refrigerator and most also have a television set and a washing machine, although only two out of every five families own a car.

◁ **How the average household budget was spent in 1986**
More than half the family budget is spent on food and housing, which is more expensive in Israel than in many Western countries. Because of high inflation, costs continue to rise every year.

▽ **Israeli currency and stamps**
The standard unit of currency in Israel is the shekel, named after an ancient Hebrew silver coin. The colourful postage stamps have the name of the country in three languages: Arabic, English and Hebrew.

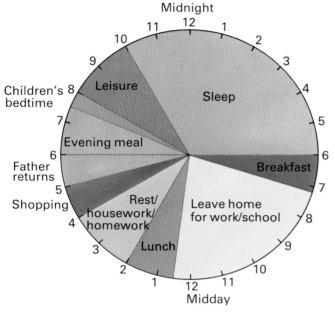

Midnight

△ **How an average family spends a working day**

▷ **What people eat**
Bread and other cereals, meat and increasingly dairy produce form the main part of people's diets, accompanied by fresh fruit and vegetables.

Bread, cereals 35%
Fats, oils 15%
Eggs, milk 11%
Meat, poultry 10%
Fruit and vegetables 9%
Potatoes 3%
Fish 1%
Others 16%

▽ **National holidays**

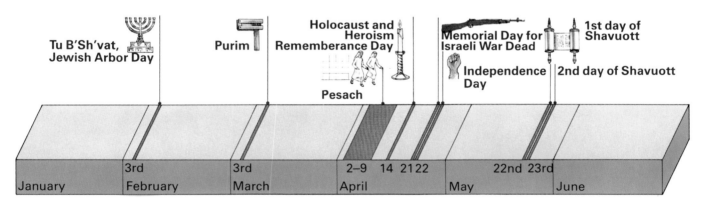

Tu B'Sh'vat, Jewish Arbor Day

Purim

Holocaust and Heroism Rememberance Day

Pesach

Memorial Day for Israeli War Dead

Independence Day

Memorial Day for Israeli War Dead | **1st day of Shavuott** | **2nd day of Shavuott**

| January | 3rd February | 3rd March | 2–9 14 21 22 April | 22nd 23rd May | June |

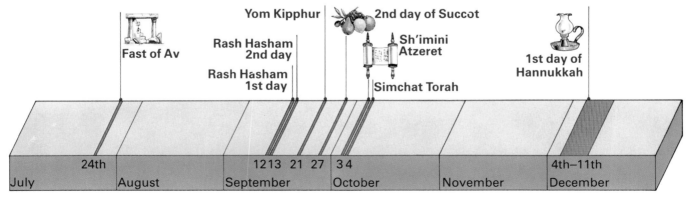

Fast of Av

Yom Kipphur

Rash Hasham 2nd day

Rash Hasham 1st day

2nd day of Succot

Sh'imini Atzeret

Simchat Torah

1st day of Hannukkah

| July | 24th August | 12 13 21 27 September | 3 4 October | November | 4th–11th December |

Farming and fishing

About 40 per cent of Israel's food requirements are imported. The remainder is produced on the country's farms, and surpluses of cash crops such as fruit (particularly oranges) and vegetables are exported to help pay for the imports.

Cereals and fruits are the major crops, with wheat the principal cereal. Cotton is also grown for the local textile industries and there is some forestry. The key to the great expansion of Israel's agriculture in the last thirty years has been the irrigation of formerly infertile desert lands and the establishment of cooperatives and collective farms called kibbutzim. Israeli agricultural scientists have also developed special strains of crops which give improved yields while at the same time tolerating the harsh desert conditions. Even so, only a little over one-fifth of the land can be farmed, and agriculture employs about 7 per cent of the workforce and contributes less than a tenth of the nation's total gross national product.

Above: Desert farming experiments are being carried out in the Negev at Wadi Navash, near Beersheba. Here a water catchment system has been set up so plum trees can be grown.

Left: Vegetables growing under plastic sheeting at Moshav Neviot, a typical cooperative farm. Israel has made its deserts fertile by means of large-scale irrigation.

Above left: Harvesting peppers by tractor at the highly mechanized Quetara Kibbutz.

Above right: A display of Israeli wines and the grapes from which they are made.

Below: An Arab tends a flock of sheep. Israeli farmers raise nearly a quarter of a million sheep for wool and meat.

Israel has passed on its farming skills and experience to many other countries, particularly those in the Third World. Since the 1950s, large numbers of agricultural students have visited Israel, and Israeli advisers have gone to other lands to help solve their farming problems.

The 3 per cent or so of Israeli Arabs who make their living in agriculture have not yet fully adopted modern farming methods. As a result, farms run as they would have been in Biblical times may be seen next to the world's most technically advanced ones.

Besides crops, Israel also raises large numbers of chickens, turkeys and beef cattle for domestic consumption. There are comparatively few sheep, while pigs are raised by few people except the Christian Arabs in the northeast of the country.

The fishing industry is based mainly on fish farms. People still fish in the Sea of Galilee, but most of their catch is eaten locally.

Natural resources and industry

Israel's natural resources are extremely limited. Its mineral deposits include bitumen, bromine, manganese, phosphates, potash and sulfur. The bromine and potash come from the salts of the Dead Sea, while the phosphates are mined in the desert of the Negev, along with some copper. The country has some magnesium. Other raw materials for industry must be imported.

As a result, Israel's industry is based largely on its scientific creativity and its ability to pioneer new technology. It has developed a chemical industry, using its minerals to produce fertilizers and drugs. It has initiated major world developments in electronics – particularly in the medical field – agricultural technology, and computer hardware and software. The main industrial center is in the Tel Aviv-Jaffa area.

Before World War II Jewish diamond cutters based in Amsterdam and Antwerp made those cities the leaders in the craft. Now Israel is also a major diamond cutting center.

Above: A cement factory at Bet Samson near Bet Shemesh, which is west of Jerusalem. The raw materials for cement making, such as gypsum and limestone, come from the Negev Desert.

Left: A chemical plant at night. Israel's chemical industry is responsible for 10 per cent of its total industrial production and 17 per cent of its industrial exports.

The country has invested heavily in scientific development. About 50,000 scientists and technologists are working at present in Israel. At least 5,000 of them are engaged in industrial research.

Israelis have to be inventive. They have had to develop their own arms industry, because traditional suppliers, such as Britain and France, stopped providing spare parts for armaments in the 1960s. One peaceful effect of the arms industry is the development of executive jet aircraft.

The production of energy is one of the country's chief problems. There is no water power, and almost no coal. The only important oil well to come under Israeli control was in the Sinai Desert. It was returned to Egypt in 1982 as part of the peace agreement with that country. Now Israel has to import most of its oil. However, its bright sunshine can provide energy, so Israel is experimenting with the best ways to harness and use solar power.

Above left: A diamond factory. Israel is a major world center for the processing of diamonds.

Above right: Circuit testing by computer. Electronics provides 13 per cent of industrial output.

Below: Shops aimed at attracting tourists in the Old City of Jerusalem. Tourism earns the country about $1,000 million every year.

The kibbutz system

Much of Israel's agriculture is based on the kibbutz system and the less well known moshav communities. Only about 3 per cent of Israel's people live on kibbutzim and 4 per cent on moshavim, but they raise most of Israel's farm produce, including cereal crops, fruit and vegetables, farm animals for meat and milk, and fish (from inland fish farms). Together they produce about a third of the country's food requirements.

The kibbutz is a collective unit, where no one has any private property. Everybody helps with the work, earnings are shared equally, and basic necessities (such as food and accommodation) are supplied by the community. People live in small, specially built houses, each with its own garden. The moshav is a cooperative in which each family and farmstead has its own property and identity. The moshav shitufi resembles a collective farm of the type common in the Soviet Union. The moshav ordim is based on the principle of equal opportunity for its members.

Above: Members of an Israeli family outside their home on the Ketjra Kibbutz. There are more than 260 kibbutzim in the country, and about 116,000 people live and work on them.

Left: Crops growing at the Engeddi Kibbutz, which is 90 metres (300 feet) above the shores of the Dead Sea. Engeddi has a good supply of fresh water from three waterfalls.

In the 1950s Israel revolutionized its agriculture by establishing a national water grid, which enabled water to be piped from the rainier north to the southern deserts. In the 1960s irrigation systems were developed. A huge reservoir of fossil water, which accumulated 30,000 years ago, is trapped under the Negev Desert. Israel is drawing on this ancient water for irrigating farm land and for industry.

Tree-planting has helped to turn marshes and deserts into good farmland. Israel exports its oranges, lemons and grapefruit under the trade name Jaffa, as well as avocados, melons and other fruit and vegetable produce under the trade name Carmel.

Israel has a free trade agreement with the European Economic Community (the Common Market). Under this it can sell industrial products to the Market duty free, and farm produce at reduced duty rates. It also has special agreements with ten other countries.

Above left: Many kibbutz families take their main meals in a large communal dining hall.
Above right: Assembly work at Beit Keset Kibbutz near Afula.

Below: A modern fish farm at the Maagan Mikhael Kibbutz in northwestern Israel, which is noted for its carp.

Transportation

In developing their transportation system the Israelis have had to bear in mind many natural obstacles and political difficulties. The biggest natural obstacle is the Negev Desert, which hinders communication between Eilat on the Gulf of Aqaba and the rest of Israel. Roads built around cease-fire lines and temporary borders have had to be redeveloped when the frontiers have changed after Israel's wars.

In the 1970s and 1980s many major roads, including the first highways, have been built, and other roads are being improved. There are now more than 600,000 private vehicles.

The most popular system of public transportation within Israel is the bus service, which extends across the Negev Desert to Eilat. The best-known operator is Egged, a co-operative company owned by the drivers themselves. These buses offer a comprehensive and fairly cheap nationwide travel network. Much quicker for inter-city travel is the sherut or communal taxi.

Above: The new highway between Jerusalem and Tel Aviv has greatly reduced travel time between these two major cities.

Below: The Egged bus system is owned entirely by its workers. It provides an economical national transportation network.

The very limited rail system is a relic of the old line built in the 1800s when Israel was part of the Ottoman (Turkish) Empire. Passenger trains run along the coast linking the major towns from Ashkelon in the south to Haifa in the north, and there is a line inland to Jerusalem, and there are freight trains to Eilat. Rail journeys are much slower than the more efficient bus travel.

Passengers are now choosing to fly around the country on internal air services. El Al, Israel's national airline, carries about 1,400,000 passengers a year throughout the world. It operates international flights from Ben Gurion Airport at Lod, near Tel Aviv. There are also international charter flights direct to airports at Jerusalem and Eilat.

Ships sail to and from Israel across the Mediterranean, up the Gulf of Aqaba to Eilat or through Egypt's Suez Canal. Eilat and the Mediterranean ports of Haifa and Ashdod have deep-water harbors for large ships. Ashkelon and Hadera are mainly industrial ports.

Above left: The Jerusalem to Tel Aviv train snakes its way through forests.

Above: El Al, the national airline, is named after a Biblical phrase meaning 'On high'.

Below: Containers lined up at Haifa, on the Mediterranean coast, ready to export more of Israel's technology.

Fact file: economy and trade

Key facts

Structure of production: Of the total gross domestic product (the GDP, or the value of all economic activity inside Israel), farming, fishing and forestry contribute 5 per cent, industry 27 per cent, and services 68 per cent.

Farming: Only 21 per cent of Israel is crop land, and nearly half of this must be irrigated; 40 per cent is grazing land; and nearly 6 per cent is forest. Israel produces 60 per cent of the food it needs. *Main products:* cereals, citrus and other fruits, cotton, grapes (for wine making), olives, vegetables. *Livestock:* cattle, 330,000; sheep, 240,000; goats, 115,000; poultry, 248,000.

Fishing: The catch in 1984 was 22,402 tonnes. Nearly 60 per cent of this came from inland waters.

Mining: Potash, bromine, magnesium and other salts from the Dead Sea area are the most valuable resources. Some oil and natural gas are also extracted, and copper, limestone and other materials are mined.

Energy: Consumption in 1985 totalled 15,000 million kWh. Most electrical energy is generated at oil-fuelled thermal stations. Much oil is imported.

Manufacturing: Major industries include the processing of farm products, textiles, chemicals and diamonds. Israel also has aircraft, electronics, machinery, metal, munitions, plastics and transportation equipment industries. The main manufacturing area is around Tel Aviv-Jaffa.

Trade (1985): *Total imports:* US $8,800 million; *exports:* $6,000 million; Israel is the sixth most important trading nation in the Middle East after Saudi Arabia, Iran, Kuwait, Iraq and Turkey.

Economic growth: The average growth rate of Israel's gross national product (GNP) between 1973 and 1983 was 1 per cent a year; the per capita GNP rose by 0.9 per cent a year in the same period.

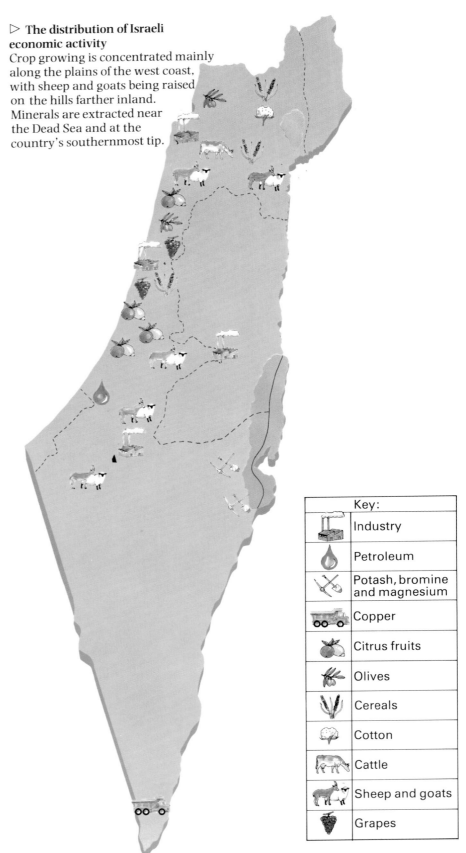

▷ **The distribution of Israeli economic activity**
Crop growing is concentrated mainly along the plains of the west coast, with sheep and goats being raised on the hills farther inland. Minerals are extracted near the Dead Sea and at the country's southernmost tip.

Key:	
	Industry
	Petroleum
	Potash, bromine and magnesium
	Copper
	Citrus fruits
	Olives
	Cereals
	Cotton
	Cattle
	Sheep and goats
	Grapes

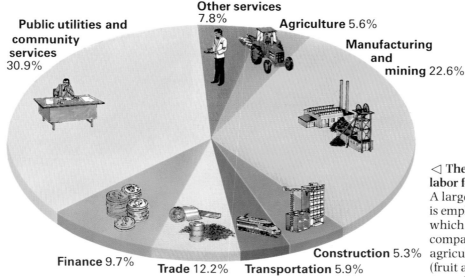

Other services 7.8%

Public utilities and community services 30.9%

Agriculture 5.6%

Manufacturing and mining 22.6%

Finance 9.7%

Trade 12.2%

Transportation 5.9%

Construction 5.3%

◁ **The distribution of the Israeli labor force by industry in 1986** A large proportion of the labor force is employed in services industries, which continue to expand, with comparatively few people working in agriculture, although the cash crops (fruit and vegetables) they produce are valuable exports.

▷ **Israel's main trading partners in 1986** Israel trades mainly with Europe and the United States, although importing much more from the Common Market (EEC) and the rest of Europe than it exports to those countries.

▽ **The composition of Israeli imports and exports in 1986** Israel's chief exports are manufactured goods and fuels and oils. The country cannot produce enough staple foods for its needs, and for this reason its imports are dominated by foodstuffs (particularly wheat).

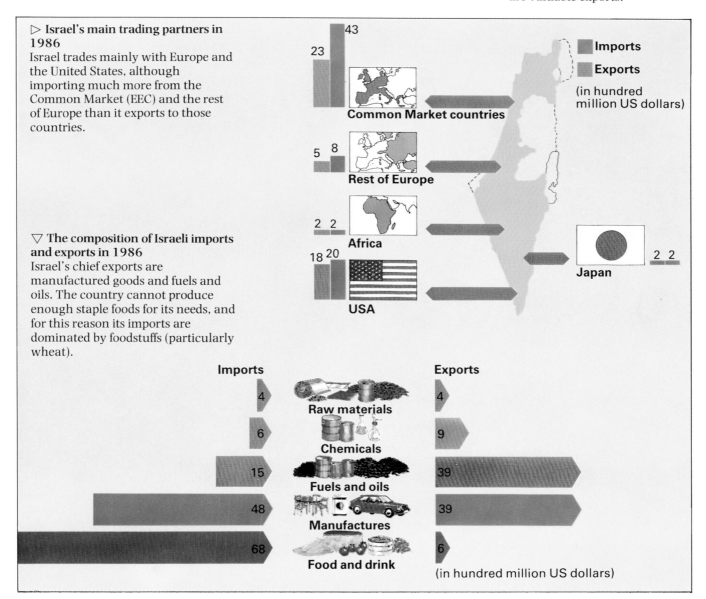

Imports

Exports

(in hundred million US dollars)

Common Market countries 23 43
Rest of Europe 5 8
Africa 2 2
USA 18 20
Japan 2 2

Raw materials — Imports 4, Exports 4
Chemicals — Imports 6, Exports 9
Fuels and oils — Imports 15, Exports 39
Manufactures — Imports 48, Exports 39
Food and drink — Imports 68, Exports 6

(in hundred million US dollars)

Education

A good education system is particularly important in Israel because of the need to bring together people from many countries and cultures. Education is free and compulsory for all children between the ages of 5 and 16. Free education is also available up to the age of 18, and more than 60 per cent of all pupils take advantage of it.

As well as the more conventional academic schools, the Ministry of Education runs technological and agricultural schools and Jewish religious academies. Immigrants who cannot speak Hebrew are encouraged to attend an ulpan, a school which provides crash courses in the language.

Three of Israel's seven universities were established in the 1920s and 1930s. The other four have been opened since Israel's independence because of the huge increase in would-be students. Institutes of higher education specialize in various fields, such as teaching, nursing, music and fine arts. The Open University offers adult education by correspondence courses, radio and television.

Above: A group of children on their way to school in the Old City of Jerusalem, carrying heavy bags of books for their studies.

Below: A lecturer takes a tutorial at the Hebrew University in Jerusalem. It is one of the oldest of Israel's seven universities.

All young Israelis – both men and women – must serve in the armed forces, where they are offered more educational opportunities.

Druzes are Arabic-speaking people whose religion is related to Islam. Because of the different needs of Jewish and Arab/Druze communities, there are two parallel school systems. In the Jewish system children are taught in Hebrew. In the Arab/Druze system they are taught in Arabic. One of the greatest successes of the Israeli education system is the increasing numbers of Arab and Druze girls who now continue into the upper years of high school. In both groups few girls used to be educated. Small schools have also been set up for nomadic Bedouin children in the Negev Desert.

Most schools are run by the government, but there are a few independent schools, run mainly by Orthodox Jewish sects and communities.

Above: A group of Armenian schoolchildren in Jerusalem, whose ancestors fled from Russia to escape persecution by the Ottoman Turks.

Below: In a Yeshiva, a religious school, Jewish men follow an intensive course of study in religious matters. It often involves vigorous discussions.

Culture and the arts

Although Israel is a young country, it has an ancient culture. The Hebrew language is several thousand years old, but from 200 A.D. to 1850 it was not widely spoken.

The first great Hebrew poet of the modern age was Chaim Nachman Bialik (1873–1934), who has been described as Israel's national poet. The novelist Shmuel Yosef Agnon (1888–1970) won the 1966 Nobel prize for literature. Israeli writers who have tried to respond to suffering under the Holocaust include such poets as Abba Kovner (1918–87) and such fiction writers as Aharon Appelfeld (1932–   ). The new writers of Israel are social critics and literary experimenters.

The visual arts are influenced by the New Horizons art movement, which for several years encouraged abstract forms of painting. Israel has not yet developed a strong national style.

Music plays a large part in the country's cultural life. There are six major orchestras, and Israel has many world-famous soloists.

Above: Chaim Bialik, one of the greatest modern Hebrew poets, greatly influenced other writers.
Below left: Shmuel Agnon was a prize-winning novelist.

Below: Music and ballet combine in Peter and the Wolf.

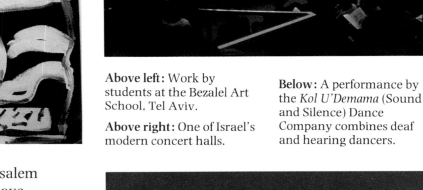

Above left: Work by students at the Bezalel Art School, Tel Aviv.

Above right: One of Israel's modern concert halls.

Below: A performance by the *Kol U'Demama* (Sound and Silence) Dance Company combines deaf and hearing dancers.

The Inbal Dance Theatre and Jerusalem Dance Company are groups which have brought together traditional European, classical Middle Eastern and modern Israeli dance styles. The Kol U'Demama (Sound and Silence) Dance Ensemble includes both deaf and hearing dancers.

The country has four repertory theater companies, which frequently go on international tours. It has a flourishing film industry which makes about a dozen full-length movies every year.

Israel has over 3,500 known archaeological sites. One of the most important is Masada, the site of Jewish resistance to the Romans in 66–73 A.D. Many finds are displayed in Israel's 80 museums. Museums of particular interest are the Shrine of the Book in Jerusalem, which houses the Dead Sea Scrolls, the Holocaust Museum (*Yad Va Shem*) in Jerusalem, and Bet Hatefutsot (the museum of the Diaspora), showing the history of Jewish communities around the world.

The making of modern Israel

Throughout the Diaspora, Jews have prayed and hoped to return to Palestine, the name by which their ancient land was known for centuries. A few Jews had remained there, and in the 19th century more and more made the hazardous journey to Palestine, then under the rule of the Ottoman Turks.

In 1897 a Hungarian-born Jewish journalist, Theodor Herzl, organized the first Zionist Congress in Switzerland. Zionists, dedicated to forming a new Jewish State in Palestine, took their name from Mount Zion in Jerusalem, which symbolized their homeland. In 1917, during World War I, the British Foreign Secretary, Arthur J. Balfour, promised British support.

In 1922, four years after the end of World War I, Britain was given a mandate to govern Palestine, which had previously been Turkish. It split the territory in two. The eastern three-quarters, called Transjordan, was placed under Arab rule, and Jews were allowed to settle in the west.

Above: Theodor Herzl, the leader of the Zionist movement, aboard ship on his way to Palestine in 1898.

Below: Early Jewish immigrants working on the land at Gedera, a settlement which was founded in 1884.

Left: The British tried to stop refugees from the Holocaust landing in Palestine, but the immigrants quickly mingled with the crowds waiting on shore and were impossible to detect.

Below: The Statesman David Ben Gurion proclaiming the new State of Israel on May 14, 1948, at a constituent assembly meeting in the Tel Aviv Museum. He became Israel's first prime minister.

The Arabs opposed Jewish immigration, and more Arabs moved into western Palestine. Britain found itself caught between Arab hostility and Jewish hopes. In 1947, after World War II, the United Nations voted to split western Palestine into two States, one Jewish, one Arab. The Jews accepted the idea, the Arabs did not, and fighting broke out. On May 14, 1948, the British withdrew, and the new Jewish State of Israel was proclaimed.

The next day troops of five Arab countries – Egypt, Iraq, Lebanon, Syria and Transjordan – attacked Israel. Fighting lasted more than a year until a ceasefire was signed in July 1949. The new Arab State in Palestine was never formed. Part of its proposed territory was held by Israel and the rest by Transjordan (now called Jordan) and Egypt. Some Palestinian Arabs stayed where they were, but nearly half a million fled to Arab lands where they were placed in refugee camps. In 1964 they founded the Palestine Liberation Organization (PLO).

Israel in the modern world

Modern Israel has fought five wars in its brief history. The most dramatic was the Six-Day War in 1967. Israel, attacked on three sides by Egypt, Syria and Jordan, repulsed its enemies so successfully that it found itself controlling lands which contained large numbers of those Palestinian Arabs who had left Israel in 1948.

Israel and Egypt negotiated a peace treaty, which was signed in March 1979. As a result, Israel handed back Sinai to Egypt, a move completed in 1982. It retained control of the disputed territories of the Gaza strip, the West Bank of the Jordan, and the Golan Heights, which assured it secure borders.

It is remarkable how significant a part Israel plays in world affairs, and how effectively it has held back its much stronger enemies for so long. What is still more remarkable is that it has succeeded in keeping its democratic and open political structure and media, despite military pressures that might have forced it to slip into military dictatorship.

Above: Israeli soldiers on guard in Sinai, between Israel and Egypt, after the Six-Day War.

Left: Israel's 1972 Olympic team mourn 11 comrades killed by PLO terrorists in Munich.

Below: President Jimmy Carter of the United States clasps hands with President Anwar Sadat of Egypt (left) and Menachem Begin of Israel (right) in 1979, as Israel makes peace with Egypt.

Israel's resourcefulness and determination have impressed the world. It has shown them in such actions as its daring rescue of Jewish hostages hijacked at Entebbe in Uganda in 1976, and its airlift of 10,000 starving Jews from famine-ridden Ethiopia in 1985.

However, until Israel resolves the problems of Arab hostility and the desire of the Palestinian Arabs to have a greater say in their own future, it will not be able to contribute to the Middle East as much as it could. Certainly the peace between Egypt and Israel offers real hope. Some experts speculate that peace between Jordan and Israel might develop, and friendly contacts have been established with a more distant Arab country, Morocco. The Israelis consider themselves ready to make difficult decisions in exchange for peace.

Meanwhile Israel faces economic problems. It has imposed heavy taxes and wage freezes to try to reduce an annual rate of inflation of 400 per cent. Despite its huge spending on defense the country provides good welfare services.

Above left: A Jewish boy who had been airlifted from famine-stricken Ethiopia in 1985.

Above right: The Soviet Jewish dissident Anatoly Scharansky arriving in Israel in 1986.

Below: The military cemetery of Har Herzl at Jerusalem is a grim reminder of the wars that Israel has fought in its years of independence, and of the tension that still persists.

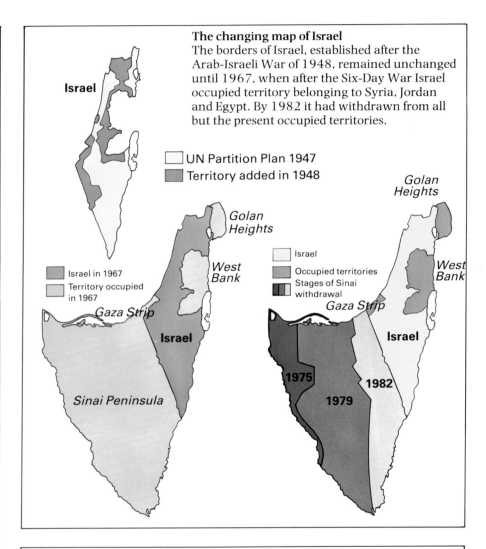

Fact file: government and world role

Key facts

Official name: *Medinat Yisra'el*, Hebrew for "State of Israel".

Flag: White, with two horizontal blue stripes. Between the two stripes is the blue *Magen David* (Shield of David).

National anthem: *Hatikvah* ("The Hope").

National government: Israel is a multi-party republic. *Head of State:* The President, who is elected to a 5-year term by the legislature. The President may serve only two terms. *Head of government:* The prime minister, who forms and heads the cabinet.

Legislature: A one-chamber parliament, the Knesset, which has 120 members elected to 4-year terms. The voting age is 18, and elections are by proportional representation.

Armed forces: Military service is compulsory for Jewish men and unmarried women. Men serve for three years. They then stay in the reserves until the age of 55. Unmarried women serve two years and may stay in the reserves until they are 34, but are usually exempt by the age of 25. Arab citizens are exempt, but may volunteer; other non-Jews are conscripted. The army, navy and air force are united under a single chief of staff. *Army:* 104,000 personnel in 1986 (on mobilization of the entire population the army has a total strength of 400,000); *Navy:* 6,600 personnel (1,000 reservists); *Air force:* 30,000 personnel. In 1982 military spending represented 25.5 per cent of the GNP (gross national product). This was four times the world average.

Economic alliances: Since 1975 Israel has had a cooperation agreement with the European Economic Community, giving it customs advantages and access to aid from the European investment Bank.

Political alliances: Israel joined the United Nations in 1949. It has close ties with the United States and receives aid from the US government.

The changing map of Israel

The borders of Israel, established after the Arab-Israeli War of 1948, remained unchanged until 1967, when after the Six-Day War Israel occupied territory belonging to Syria, Jordan and Egypt. By 1982 it had withdrawn from all but the present occupied territories.

- ▢ UN Partition Plan 1947
- ▨ Territory added in 1948

Israel

Golan Heights

- ▨ Israel in 1967
- ▢ Territory occupied in 1967

Gaza Strip

Israel

Sinai Peninsula

West Bank

Golan Heights

- ▢ Israel
- ▨ Occupied territories
- ▨ Stages of Sinai withdrawal

Gaza Strip

Israel

West Bank

1975 **1982**

1979

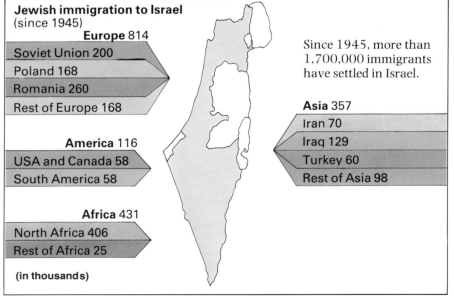

Jewish immigration to Israel (since 1945)

Europe 814

| Soviet Union 200 |
| Poland 168 |
| Romania 260 |
| Rest of Europe 168 |

America 116

| USA and Canada 58 |
| South America 58 |

Africa 431

| North Africa 406 |
| Rest of Africa 25 |

Since 1945, more than 1,700,000 immigrants have settled in Israel.

Asia 357

| Iran 70 |
| Iraq 129 |
| Turkey 60 |
| Rest of Asia 98 |

(in thousands)

Government structure

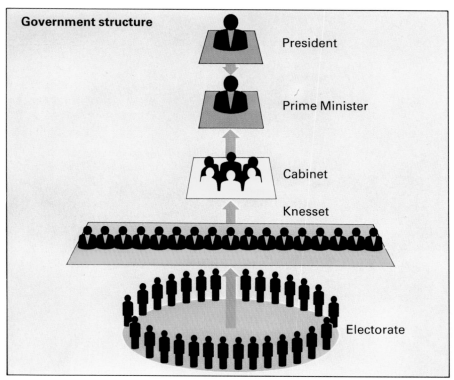

President

Prime Minister

Cabinet

Knesset

Electorate

◁ **The Israeli government**
The President is elected for a five-year term and the government run by a Prime Minister and Cabinet, chosen by the Knesset (parliament) which is elected by proportional representation for a maximum of four years.

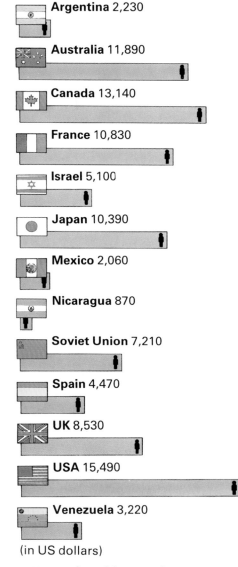

Argentina 2,230

Australia 11,890

Canada 13,140

France 10,830

Israel 5,100

Japan 10,390

Mexico 2,060

Nicaragua 870

Soviet Union 7,210

Spain 4,470

UK 8,530

USA 15,490

Venezuela 3,220

(in US dollars)

△ **National wealth created per person in 1986**
Israel is not a wealthy nation compared with most countries of Western Europe, which it relies on for trade and international support, or the nearby oil-rich Arab states of the Middle East.

▽ **Israel's neighbors**
Israel has borders with five Arab nations – Lebanon, Syria, Jordan and Egypt – with all of which it has fought wars in the last twenty years. Most of these, as well as other Arab countries, support the Palestine Liberation Organization (PLO) which continues its struggle to establish an Arab nation in territory now occupied by Israel.

TURKEY

CYPRUS

SYRIA

LEBANON

IRAQ

ISRAEL

JORDAN

EGYPT

SAUDI ARABIA

Index